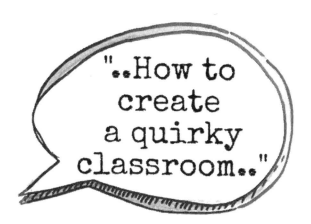

"..How to
create
a quirky
classroom.."

By

Gemma Whitelock

ISBN: 1547151994
ISBN 13: 9781547151998

"A book for all of the positive people in 'Education Land'... **Know that you are appreciated and that what you do is AMAZING!**"

"..A special
mention has to go
to my kids, **Ruby
and Ben,** a
constant test of
my patience and
creativity...
Without whom this
book would have
been finished a
lot sooner!"

x

Contents

A little note about me

Okay. So you've probably already noticed that I'm a bit of a random creative. I do seem to draw and colour in everything (I mean seriously, I was one of those kids who would have been a teachers worst nightmare... I was a doodler!) Before you start to read this book and 'listen' to my humble ramblings on teaching ...I thought it would be good to introduce myself. So you can kind of get the measure of me and see what I'm about before you step into my weird world of doodles, resources and general teaching 'stuff'...

#01 I have a penchant for laminating and have blogged about how similar laminating is to meditating... Oohhmmm

#02 I am slightly obsessed with Harry Potter… Still waiting for a job to pop up on the TES for Hogwarts.

#03 I can't relax. Like never.. I often get told off for not switching off.

#04 I spend too much time on Twitter and Pinterest.

#05 Paperchase is the best shop ever. Not up for debate.

#06 I feed my staff cake to make them happy and motivated. It's a tried and tested leadership strategy.

#07 I often make excuses for buying more trainers when really there is no excuse needed... After all, there is no such thing as too many pairs (this is often a rumor wheeled out by those with ugly feet.)

#08 Anyone can buy me with post it notes, although they do have to be very nice colours (wine also works!)

A little note about this book

This book will let you in on the things that I have developed during my time researching for my MA in Education. Over that period I had the opportunity to do that thing that very few of us teacher folk feel that we have the time to do... I had the chance to genuinely and legitimately play, test out, refine resources and develop new engaging approaches to my teaching practice. With the help of my students (who were always keen to be experimented on and voice their often opinionated views on my new ideas) I developed a range of strategies that have proved to work for a range of areas within my classroom practice.

Over the last few years I have shared lots of resources on Twitter and also with pretty much anyone who asks nicely (or makes payment in post it notes, although this is not always necessary. As mentioned previously, wine is also accepted as payment.) My philosophy on this kind of thing is always along the lines of, "why keep a good thing to yourself!?" ...When something works I reckon it's rude not to share. This job is hard enough with all of the external pressures imposed upon us. So here is my contribution to the team... For you to read, download, edit and adapt for you own needs, anything to make things that little bit easier.

This book is a snapshot of me and my teaching methods. There are copies of my quirky resources included ready for you to edit and make suitable for your own teaching groups. All of the strategies and resources featured can easily be edited for use across the full spectrum of education stages... After all, everyone learns better when the resources and teaching tools are visually engaging and a little bit quirky, regardless of their level of learning.

A note on QR codes

I will discuss the wonder of QR codes a little later... However, you will notice that there are such codes scattered throughout the book. These unlock a direct link to the resource templates and examples that are discussed in each section of the book.

The links will work best on a device with a large screen so that you can view the content and edit. The resources all live in a 'Quirky Classroom' Dropbox folder in various different formats ready for you to edit... Make sure that you save them in your personal documents before editing.

If you prefer to go 'old school' and type a link into your web browser, there are full web links next to each QR code for you to type onto the inter-web so that you can share in the same loveliness.

Scan the code to access the full range of 'Quirky Classroom' downloads.
https://www.dropbox.com/s h/ua5gr1uv1qttbux/AAAU1il ZWQUtA-6imFtebGs6a?dl=0

The 'Quirky Classroom' Commandments

Before we commence in sharing the quirkiness… There are a couple of little things that will help you to play the game.

#01 You must be open to the experimental nature of these resources. Just because they work for me and lots of others, doesn't necessarily mean that they will work *fresh out of the box* for you and your cohort of learners... This is why they are available for you to download, edit and refine as needed for YOUR own teaching.

#02 You must be ready for the daftness and potential for people (usually other very boring colleagues who have delivered the curriculum in the same way for YEARS) to look at you like you have slightly lost the plot. Believe me when I tell you that this is a normal reaction. As long as the learning is sticking as a direct result of your new slightly bonkers methods... Who cares!?

NB: as a side note, being referred to as 'weird' (or other local variation of the same word) is a normal part of adopting the elements of the 'Quirky Classroom' ethos. The students are likely to have such opinions initially until they realise that the 'weird' they are experiencing is actually making their lessons with you become much more interesting. As for any staff that make similar comments... What can I say people... haters gonna hate.

..and another thing

Please don't try and sell any of the resources in this book (either before or after you have added any of your content) on any of the various online 'resource meat markets'... By all means share with colleagues, friends, family and anyone who wants to listen. But selling is just not cricket and it's not okay with me... Okay? *Insert teacher death stare and wagging finger here * ahem.

Thank you muchly x

#LiteracyGames

In a climate where students use abbreviated 'text speak' as their everyday language, it is an uphill struggle to get the 'literacy stuff' right... **Let's face it; we are just as bad - what with our WAGOLLS, IEP's, SOW and the like, us teachers LOVE a good acronym too!** However, I digress... Before the delights of work that lie ahead for our students (where such acronyms will be commonplace and help them to impress colleagues with their best David Brent impression) *we* have the slightly pressured job of ensuring that we are maintaining the standards of written work to get them employed (as well as covering the curriculum stuff along the way too.) **Hands up if you've heard the phrase '*We are all teachers of literacy!?*'...** *Yep, thought so!*

Okay, so we all know about literacy and the increased need to get more quality into the written work within our subjects. Regardless of what subject area you teach, there's always an assessed written element to it. In my experience as a teacher of a practical subject area, it was always a struggle to get students to understand the importance of the written element to their work. It was always an afterthought at best and often added in a rush at the 11th hour. **As an art teacher that dreaded comment from a year 11 student the day before the coursework deadline... 'I've done everything Miss, just need to do my annotations!'** ...As if they could suddenly remember *the entire* intricate fine details of their experimentation and development process to be able to discuss their work to the standard that was needed before tomorrow morning!

From working with students across KS3 and KS4, trying to unpick the issues within this area has given some interesting outcomes that can help to develop other areas of the curriculum too.

The Game Plan

It makes sense, all of the things that create the barriers to students developing good literacy pretty much stem from the place.. It needs to be a steady progression with structure and support in place along the whole journey but it needs to have a little consideration for the 'customers' as well.. **Everyone can do a writing frame and a spelling test to tick the literacy box. If you want to get the students to truly 'buy in' to the importance of developing literacy in your subject area, you need to include an element of fun.**

So, on a mission to get more fun into the written elements of my lessons, work began to develop things to help the students feel more 'okay' with the concept of writing in Art. **There were some rather amusing epic fails in my quest to get literacy a bit more exciting.. Namely the paper planes with extended questioning on them — that was utter chaos!** And so, I shall save you dear reader the trouble (and total mortifying embarrassment of paper plane chaos) by letting you in on my top tips for improving the quality of student's written work without them even noticing it!

Loyalty Cards

Use keywords & stretch students further!

If you think about the things that you value, the things that make you as a consumer get 'on board' with a certain shop or brand... It's the little things. The way that they market their stuff and give you a little perks for being a loyal customer.

Take coffee shop loyalty cards for example... Buying 10 items gets you some sort of 'treat'. What if we did this for the students at school? **What if they used certain words, connectives or topics of conversations within their work numerous times and we re-warded them for it?**

This is exactly how the literacy loyalty cards work. It is essentially a nicely presented list of keywords or phrases that are needed to enhance the student's level of working. The more that they use, the more they are showing loyalty to their learning. **They simply tick off the ones they have used in one particular piece of work or over a certain period of time and are rewarded** (you know, with merits, sweets and the like) for their efforts.

These have been a real eye opener in my classes - and even created a competitive edge to written work! **The lists also provide fabulously easy homework tasks as spelling revision too!**

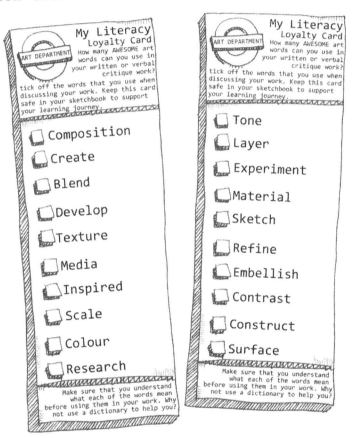

Scan the code to access the 'Literacy Loyalty Card' downloads and templates for editing yourself.

https://www.dropbox.com/sh/dt t5uyr7roomi3y/AACUpNAzg1WZJZa SeWcEgdUHa?dl=0

Literacy Balls

This is a bit more of an energetic one... and **a good way to pop a bit of verbal literacy into your lesson.** The balls that work best for this are the football style ones with the different sections clearly stitched into the design. At an appropriate reflection point within the lesson - particularly if it is part way through a practical session or maybe part way through a particularly intense written lesson - the students

So simple but so effective!

work in small groups and throw one of the literacy balls between them.

When they catch the ball, they use the word/question nearest to their thumb to prompt reflection on their progress or to peer assess the work of others.

Make it work for you...

#01 Try using **subject key words** on the different sections of the balls.

#02 Use **Blooms taxonomy to encourage higher order questioning**... Brilliant for KS4 and KS5 groups to get them thinking about exam technique.

#03 Or... If you want them to work for a number of subjects or topic areas, **why not use numbers or colours to correspond with an additional worksheet with coded questions, words or themes for each task?**

Literacy Jenga

Labelled up & ready for a game!

This game was one of the early additions to the 'teaching toy box'— to my amazement, it just worked. **One of those moments when you're mooching around the toy section during the food shop looking at games and trying to work out how you can use it to make literacy more engaging... I know I'm such a nerd.**

Admittedly this was one of those things that I thought was a little bit bonkers (yes... even I thought that the Jenga may have been a step too far!) but my mission for fun forced me to have a go anyway! What's the worst that could happen? Surely this couldn't have been as bad as the paper planes!?

This one REALLY is brilliant and so adaptable for lots of different subjects. So, how does it work? Each Jenga brick has a word written on it. The students work in small groups and play the game as normal. BUT.. Every time that they remove a brick, they write the word down for later use in their written work.

The game works well as a starter for a written lesson. My exam groups have enjoyed using it, particularly when they get into a bit of writing rut and struggle for inspiration with their annotations and review of their practical work.

Use some supportive resources to model how you want the Jenga words used in their work.

Try to work through one example as a group/class before allowing independent work and full game play!

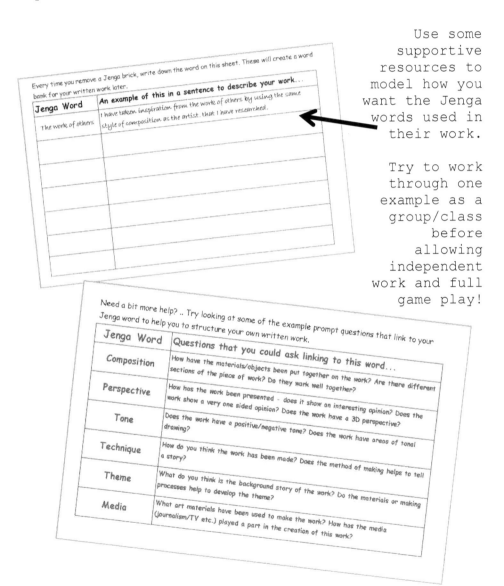

Every time you remove a Jenga brick, write down the word on this sheet. These will create a word bank for your written work later.

Jenga Word	An example of this in a sentence to describe your work...
The work of others	I have taken inspiration from the work of others by using the same style of composition as the artist that I have researched.

Need a bit more help? .. Try looking at some of the example prompt questions that link to your Jenga word to help you to structure your own written work.

Jenga Word	Questions that you could ask linking to this word...
Composition	How have the materials/objects been put together on the work? Are there different sections of the piece of work? Do they work well together?
Perspective	How has the work been presented - does it show an interesting opinion? Does the work show a very one sided opinion? Does the work have a 3D perspective?
Tone	Does the work have a positive/negative tone? Does the work have areas of tonal drawing?
Technique	How do you think the work has been made? Does the method of making helps to tell a story?
Theme	What do you think is the background story of the work? Do the materials or making processes help to develop the theme?
Media	What art materials have been used to make the work? How has the media (journalism/TV etc.) played a part in the creation of this work?

Scan the code to access the 'Jenga game sheet' download template for editing yourself as well as example PowerPoint presentations.
https://www.dropbox.com/sh/lgayezxkhylgj99/AADqEMvZoPs5Qo-j5h-VGB5Ca?dl=0

Try it this way...

As a starter task — ask **students to write a description of a particular piece of work.** Maybe they peer assess the work of someone else in the group. It is important that students do this before the Jenga game...

Then, **play the literacy Jenga game using a worksheet to support the task.** When students have their list of words, ask them to create sentences to describe or provide feedback on the work that they used at the start of the lesson.

Ask students to compare difference in written content before and after playing jenga... Voila — Clear progress!

Keyword Bingo

This game really is minimum effort, maximum engagement. My KS3 groups LOVED BINGO! **This one was a real game changer for me. So often as the teacher of a practical subject the students would dread written lessons.** The mere mention of the word 'evaluation' would switch them off.. Using this as a starter gets them on board and excited about written lessons.

"Eyes down for a full house!"

If you have the cards printed and ready, all you need is a few prizes... Whatever currency works for your groups (merits, stickers, sweets or maybe even post its... **Yes I did have a group of year 8 who loved post it's as much as me!)**

Simply play the game, collecting words that correspond to the numbers on the game card. Then use the words within the written task.

Scan the code to access the 'Keyword Bingo' templates for you to save and edit as well as an example PowerPoint to help run the game.
https://www.dropbox.com/sh/u8k xj0ewxzqzir9/AAA5VOoUmr2honmek CSoRrla?dl=0

It works well to keep the competitive theme going through out the lesson. Why not give extra rewards for students who use all of their words?

Top Tip...

Make life a bit easier — create a slideshow with relevant keywords that correspond to the bingo numbers. REALLY easy to edit the words each time you need to change the topic or focus of the written task. Just shuffle up the order of the numbers and click through one slide at a time... Simple!

KEYWORD BINGO

01	12	04	07	19
11	14	15	06	03

HOW IT WORKS... Listen for your numbers. Cross out the number when its called - but also **write down the keyword that is called out onto your whiteboard.** If you cross all of your numbers out shout BINGO!

KEYWORD BINGO

20	05	09	01	19
08	14	15	17	13

HOW IT WORKS... Listen for your numbers. Cross out the number when its called - but also **write down the keyword that is called out onto your whiteboard.** If you cross all of your numbers out shout BINGO!

Traveller information: Expanding your vocabulary

10
Research

Traveller information: Expanding your vocabulary

17
Composition

The bingo game cards have different combinations of the different keywords in the game.

You just need to allocate a keyword to each number from 1-20 then you are all set to play!

Need a quick fix to 'pep up' what you currently do?

Just thinking about how you present your resources can make all the difference to the way that students engage with them... Why not use an app to create your resources, reference to popular culture or use COLOUR to make them more visually exciting?
..If the idea of printing colour stuff is too costly just do a class set and laminate them so you can re-use them (yup - I said the 'L' word, permission to crack the laminator out! What's not to love!?)

Things to remember for successful literacy

#TopTip

..look for cheap games in pound shops and along the toy aisles in the supermarket. You'd be amazed how inspiration can strike in the least likely of places!
Or..**Why not download the templates included with this book and get your 'literacy game' on now!?**

#01 Think about your resources like you're marketing a brand. The one thing that hooks the students in is something that they can relate to. That's why the games work. They are familiar and fun.

#02 Make things accessible - try to make the support materials as user friendly as possible.. Think about the size and shape of the materials you are producing might sound a little obvious but it's often forgotten!

#03 Make it enjoyable and make it fun for you too. If you're the kind of person who has a bit of a penchant for twister.. Why not go for it and adapt it into a literacy game!?

Okay, so what if the game stuff is a step too far for you? (what can I say, I did warn you that the ideas would be categorised under 'weird')

..There are a few examples of literacy mats and support cards like these that may be useful to spark inspiration for your own creations..

Mini Train Ticket literacy support

Scan the QR code to access 'Literacy Mat Examples'
https://www.dropbox.com/sh/a2imellaz0c7bv3/ AACSOhL5Nbmw_UboBhWReMmva?dl=0

#Makingitreal

With such a huge emphasis on work experience and getting students 'workplace ready' it only seems right that we embed as much of this as we can during our time in the classroom. Having decided to make it a personal mission of mine a few years ago (it was a slight moment of madness when planning the summer term) I thought it was only fair to share the experiences and also squeeze my top tips into this little section of the book.

The #makingitreal 'thing' is about creating as many real life opportunities for the students as possible... **Experience of the workplace doesn't have to be a week-long placement in a crisp factory in year 10...** Although that would be rather brilliant, imagine all of the freebies! (Note to self: must explore crisp factory jobs)..**Simply popping little nuggets of 'realness' into the design of the curriculum at appropriate moments has just as much impact.** Particularly if these opportunities are scattered through the lower years of school, this way we can ensure that there is a constant feeling of 'doing something real' and generally getting ready for life after the classroom into the big scary world of being a grown up and having a job.

Throughout this section you will find case studies linked to the different ways that you can adopt the #makingitreal ethos within your own classroom... They are my 'best bits' from the year-long mission and will hopefully inspire you to think a little differently when curriculum planning and teaching the 'quirky classroom' way.

Look for an Audience

Never underestimate the power of a 'real' audience for the work that your students produce... Whether it be a prominent space in the main area of school or a space used by a wider audience in the local community. Knowing that their work will be seen by people beyond the classroom walls really helps to improve the

Sharing with the community

quality of what is produced as well as the overall work ethic of the group.

This is something that undoubtedly in a creative subject is a lot easier (and maybe slightly gives us arty types the edge) as we obviously have lots of visual 'stuff' to show. However, with the right audience a really well presented project or length of written work is just as attractive. Think about all of the historical artefacts that people read through in museums ...People like to read as well as look at pictures!

Try it this way...

#01 Present work during open evenings or parents evenings.. Take a leaf out of the art department book and think about how you present the pieces to the audience. Less is more when it comes to display. I'm all for a colourful notice board, but when it comes to a display of work to a wider audience you need to think a little more like a gallery or museum curator. Keep the background clean and neutral. Let the work speak for itself. Just make sure there is a title and explanation for the work presented to set the context.

#02 Ask local spaces and places if they have any opportunities to display work created by local schools. You would be surprised how many places actually need to provide evidence that they are actively engaging with the education sector... this type of activity ticks their box just nicely!

#03 Pop a comments book out next to the work to ask for feedback from your audience on the work presented. Any comments are usually really positive... share these with your class and watch the 'happy' fill the room.

#04 Try it virtually... Does your school have the option of an online sharing forum on the website? Or maybe they are even more tech savvy and do social media like grown-ups... if this is the case, why not pop some work online to engage with an even wider audience? Just remember to channel your inner Instagram photographer when you snap the work. Check your lighting, think about your choice of background and use a filter if needed to show the work in its best light.

Case Study: End of year showcase

After a bit of local research wandering around various places over the summer holiday with my own kids, I discovered that there was an opening for an end of academic year 'schools out' display at a local nature reserve. Being a bit cheeky I enquired as to how we would get our school to be featured the following year... And so the mission started. This was the first of many cheeky 'asks' that just seemed to pay off.

The work produced over the whole academic year across all year groups was curated in an exclusive display within the local community for the whole summer holiday. **It was such a positive experience for the school and acted as a brilliant marketing strategy as well as the much needed confidence boost for lots of students whose work was featured.** Best of all, the whole thing was free. Just a little investment of time was needed to pull it all off… what's not to love!?

Get Networking

You will notice this is a common theme within my teaching ...Using Twitter as a tool to promote the teaching and learning in my classroom has been a total revelation.

Engaging with the artist

There are too many occasions to count where I have managed to connect with artists or companies who have directly inspired and influenced my planning. It's such a simple way to make the learning that little bit more real.

Case Study: Making Contact

The image above shows the snapshot of one of the Twitter exchanges between me and Kathy Dalwood (a contemporary sculptor.) We used Dalwood's work as inspiration for our year 9 3D project after she had exhibited locally. A few simple shots of the developing work shared with the artist online resulted in lots of positive comments as well as a feature on her own website.

Finding ways to make things that little bit more relevant for the students - like being able to contact the actual person who their work is based on - Really made them focus on the quality of their work. It was amazing to see the reluctant year 9 artists bothered about their work because it was being used for a 'proper' website!

Planning for employment

We are all in this teaching game for a reason... (apart from the mystical notion that we get good holidays) If you too are on my wavelength, we are all here to prepare the students that we teach for the outside world, to prepare them for employment and life beyond the safe and predictable environment of the classroom.

In my subject area it couldn't be more important. I often get enthusiastic students wanting to be fashion designers because they are really keen on shopping ...In reality, even if they actually had the necessary design skills, would they manage the workload? **Is it right for me to just teach them the specification and then send them on their way blissfully unaware of the harsh reality of the REAL design world!?**

This has caused me to do some thinking over the last couple of years. A career in design is hard work. I speak from experience, freelance work is difficult to sustain and then even if you manage to get the Holy Grail and obtain a permanent position at a high street retailer, it is often a lot less glamorous as it initially seems. I have a friend who after years of hard graft, works for a well-known menswear brand designing different blue striped shirt fabrics & has to present them enthusiastically EVERYDAY!

One of the key reasons that the work experience thing is a necessity, particularly in the more senior section of secondary school, is to ensure that we are providing students with the necessary resilience to manage the reality of employment. It's not just about browsing through the UCAS website in the summer term of year 12 and picking the 'nice looking' courses... Actually getting students ready for what is out there in their chosen pathway, getting a reality check and a good dollop of #makingitreal is what benefits them more.

Case Study: Presenting to the client

Professional design pitching for year 12

I wanted to do something new, something real with one of my 6th form groups to test the #makingitreal concept. To make this happen I set up a project that involved designing for a local client. Writing the project with the local business as the focus meant that the project felt real right from the start. The year 12 Textiles group were set the task of presenting their design outcomes to the owner of Doddington Hall and staff (after using their summer sculpture exhibition as inspiration.) After just one term of developing design skills, professional presentation methods and getting to grips with their new course in the safe environment of the classroom... They were now pitching their fashion scarves to a real client to potentially be sold in their shop to visitors... A pretty 'real' experience.

I have to say, they did me proud. A few were quite nervous with the prospect of discussing their ideas and design concepts with someone REAL. However, they soon settled in and were happily chatting away in no time. Even though it was quite difficult, I stood back and let them take the lead. It was important for them to jump in and see if they could swim rather than me speaking for them... For anyone who knows me, I quite like to talk – so this was a massive challenge!

On the way back to school there was a real confidence and sense of accomplishment. The experience gave them so much by building the foundations of their future careers in the design industry and an increased awareness of their creative skills before embarking on some really quite competitive university interviews later that year.

Try it this way...

#01 Look a little closer to home for people to give your students that 'real' workplace experience. Try asking the school governors to see if they could work with you to create a project or do a series of mock interviews. The concept works best with the element of going out to a real business... This is what makes the experience feel that bit more real instead of just completing the tasks fully in the school environment (even if they are set by someone external.)

#02 Plan ahead and look through the details of your curriculum. Think about which areas could benefit from this different approach to planning. Use other staff in the department and plan together... Splitting the task of contacting potential local businesses with the agreed project proposal will make this a lot less stressful!

Do it for Charity

I am yet to find a charity who hasn't been enthusiastic and keen for collaboration... Whether it be donations of money, practical objects or design/written work... There have always been ways to embed a little charity within my teaching. Just like the other elements of this chapter, it just needs a little extra thought at the planning stage. Working with charities and local community groups doesn't have to be the 'extra' fluffy PSHE thing that is classed as enrichment. Why not merge it in with the learning opportunities?

Case Study: 'I am Supercapes'

I came across @iamsupercapes on twitter (where else!?) and was really keen to get something going at school to support the fabulous work of this relatively fledgling charity. A few tweaks to the usual KS3 'design and make' D&T project turned into a really meaningful learning experience for the students involved. During the project they researched the charity and its purpose before starting on their own design development for 'super hero capes'.

The students were so enthusiastic with the project that homework was even completed to a better standard with extra research and modelling of ideas completed to inform their class work.

Year 9 proudly modelling their creations

They learnt to work more economically with recycled materials and developed skills to enable them to work as an effective team to make sure that the capes were produced to a good standard before we posted them off to the charity.. **For them, knowing that their work would benefit others was a real motivator.**

This project really created a spark of excitement in the textiles room and re-engaged the students with the importance of producing quality work. There is no good reason why it shouldn't work for any other subject - get researching and look for a charity or community project that fits your curriculum!

Try it this way...

Always on a mission to squeeze in a bit more?... If you are doing a charity project with KS2 or KS3 students, why not add in a little literacy opportunity too? As an added extra for the 'Supercapes' project, students wrote letters to Blue Peter to explain their work and share what they had created for the charity... **A few weeks later and lots of year 9 students were spotted around school proudly wearing their Blue Peter badges on blazer lapels.. Lots of cool points were earned amongst fellow students** (as well as staff who were quite a bit jealous as they were now way too old to get a Blue Peter badge) This helped the feel good factor of the project, especially when they realised how many free things they could get with their Blue Peter card.

Encourage them to react to the world

We all know that the latest OFSTED requirements ask us to embed 'British values' into our teaching and learning. Like many of you I immediately thought 'how the heck do I do that as well as everything else I need to fit in!?'

There are so many layers within our subjects that lend themselves brilliantly to discussion around the core British Values... Steering topics to more current and relevant news stories (obviously being sensitive to the age of the group you teach) can be a good starting point. However, what if you created a whole project that ticked lots of British Values opportunities and resulted in something 'real' shared with the community?

Case Study: 'Remembrance Poppies'

A bit of thinking and clear headspace over the summer resulted in a pang of inspiration... "Why not link a project to remembrance?" So the autumn term unfolded with each year 7 student concluding their diagnostic Art project with the creation of an individual clay poppy. This was the result of independent home learning to gather visual research, information on the Tower of London installation, the historical significance of the poppy as well as drawing tasks to fully understand the form and shape of the poppy before sculpting. The students really engaged with the project as it felt familiar to them (they had all had a good grounding from our lovely primary colleagues!) This made the introduction of new materials and the process of assessment that little bit easier.

EVERY student had work displayed to the public

The project took a whole new direction when (as usual) after seeing how brilliant the work was looking, I decided to be a bit cheeky and pester people in the local area for a space for exhibiting the work. I thought big - where else but the cathedral right? I totally expected their response to be along the lines of 'thank you but no thank you'... How wrong I was! **So the offer was a 2 week display period across Remembrance weekend at actual Lincoln cathedral... AMAZING!**

The display of the work wasn't the easiest if I'm honest. There were moments when I REALLY thought I'd bitten off more than I could chew due to the huge difference in temperature (not to mention the dramatic journey over cobbles to deliver the work!) ... As all art teachers will know, air drying clay may be cheap and cheerful but not so much fun when trying to do anything remotely ambitious with it!! But all went well in the end. Our brand new year 7's in particular were buzzing about their work being on display in such a phenomenal setting. Every student had their work included in the display... Just over 200 poppies went to the cathedral, such a perfect setting for their work. As a lovely extra the perfectly brilliant staff gave every student a free family entry to the cathedral to be able to see their work in situ for the remembrance period.

The lovely comments made by visitors really made the hard work worthwhile. Naturally, the world of Twitter provided an excellent platform for feedback; the school had their own special hashtag for the event to gather comments as a virtual alternative to a traditional visitor's book.

The students got so much out of the process and it was lovely to include the younger students in such a public exhibition so early in their school career. I think we pretty much met the criteria for 'BRITISH VALUES' with this one Mr OFSTED #JOBDONE

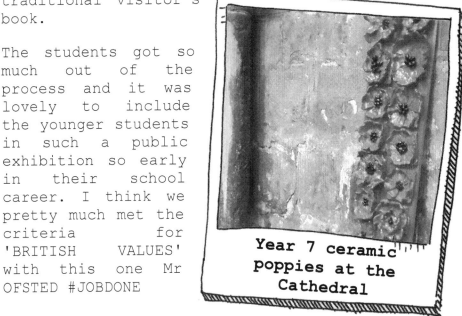

Year 7 ceramic poppies at the Cathedral

Be the proud teacher

A little name check from the editor

Ok... So you know when you get those moments when things get a little carried away and because you are a total victim of your own enthusiasm you just go along with it!? Maybe it's just me... This next case study is proof if ever there was the need for it that doing the 'proud teacher' thing totally pays off. Much the same as I do with my own kids, I do feel the need to share the positive things and amazing work that my students do. Whether it be with parents, fellow staff or in a wider arena.. It helps promote that feeling of 'job satisfaction' and general positivity that can all too often get forgotten in amongst the daily grind.

Case Study: Getting published!

One of the projects on the mission for #makingitreal with the students was for year 8 to create still life illustrations and paintings suitable for publishing in a magazine... We had used Waitrose kitchen magazine as inspiration for the project because of their lovely hand drawn illustrations. The intended end point of the project was to be a mock-up of an article with illustrations popped in using Photoshop... Allowing students to develop IT design skills too.

I was so impressed with the quality of the work produced by my students, so naturally I did what I do every other day ...I shared them on Twitter. More specifically I shared them with @williamsitwell the editor of Waitrose Kitchen magazine. To my surprise, he replied saying he was 'very impressed'...Then the project developed a whole new life of its own! **What was meant to be a fictional illustration project set up to help the students to engage in their learning actually ended up as a project for Waitrose magazine ....Literally love the power of Twitter!**

With careful planning we worked with a select group of students keen to get involved with the 'real project'. They were set the task of illustrating a very specific list of ingredients to accompany the recipes to be printed in the magazine. The biggest challenge was meeting the deadline for the publishers... Something that the students hadn't realised before would be as short as it was! The team produced some really lovely work and spent hours perfecting their illustrations in their tight turnaround time

Year 8 illustration ready for publishing

for the publishing deadline. It really was a taste of how art is applied in the real world - something that I don't think the students will ever forget. The group involved gained so much confidence as a result of the process and this has benefitted their approach to their class work too.

After submitting the illustrations to the magazine ...We played the waiting game. Even though the project was promised to be mentioned in the magazine - knowing how cut throat the publishing industry is I genuinely had no idea if many of the images that we submitted would be used. We were quite careful to prepare the students for this eventuality so they didn't feel disappointed if their hard work wasn't featured.

To my surprise, when the May issue of Waitrose Kitchen magazine arrived in store I was AMAZED to see that our work was featured on the first page! Even more surprising was the discussion in the editor's letter where I got a name check and the project was explained to the readers... **I literally couldn't have asked for a better outcome. The hard work and extra effort put in by our fabulous students had really paid off.** It really is something that has shown them (and the others around them) how with a little nurturing and direction that even they can become published illustrators at the age of 12... Just imagine what they can achieve in years to come- can't wait to find out... Total #proudteacher moment!

#TopTip

#01 Plan WAY ahead... Being organised is the key to success with this. Look for opportunities coming up locally as well as national themes and competitions to get involved with.

..How to start **#makingitreal in your classroom**

#TopTip

#02 Get on Twitter and follow the people who are relevant to your subject area. Try to start a positive conversation and share some of the work you are doing. You might be surprised what comes out of one little tweet!

#TopTip

#03 Get the Students excited about it... The fact that they are working on a 'real life' project helps to improve work quality and effort.

Remember to keep Positive... The time invested totally pays off in the end!

#TopTip

#04 Think about who to approach... who would also benefit from working with you on a project? Look for local businesses and charities that need to engage with the education sector to plan a project with.

#AWESOMEapps

The hand drawn comic style templates are one of my favourite ways of adding a bit of character to my resources (let's be honest, it's a good excuse for me to have a doodle and call it work!)However, if you aren't the arty type, there are so many fabulous apps out there that can help you to create the same personalised feel to your resources and teaching methods without an art degree. These are my personal favourites and my 'go to' apps for planning, teaching and assessing. I do not profess to be any kind of expert on such things, I have merely 'wombled' along and discovered a few hidden elements of genius that my phone and iPad can be used for in a more productive way instead of 1-click ordering on a certain well-known website... And so, here I present to you – my top 10 'Awesome Apps.'

The ideal App for **'Putting ideas out there'**

This really is an app for the technophobic people who feel a little baffled by all of the coding and alien language that was once needed to build a website (I do include myself in this by the way.. I knew people at university who did coding as part of their course...
Totally out of my comfort zone!)

The beauty of the Wordpress app is that it has so many options to personalise the sites and to pretty much make the website into any form or visual theme that you wish. The good thing about Wordpress is that the range of themes available to use when building your own site are so varied, you can edit and publish things so simply without the need to be particularly creative.. The theme and its functions do it for you.

Now... Why am I going on about building websites? Surely some ICT web designer specialist does that on behalf of the school/college right? Well yes, to be honest, the purpose of me talking about the Wordpress app is not to inspire you to take over the school website. The use of this app within my own teaching has been a little bit of a revelation. Admittedly, I have only really fully tested this within my exam groups (KS4 and above) although the use of blogs as a learning tool has been brilliant... **Teenagers as a species in my experience are often glued to their phones. They are regularly to be found snapping endless photographs to document their every detail of their dinner/make up/latest shoe purchase as well as (usually too frequently) sharing their thoughts on pretty much everything via social media.. Sounding familiar?** Now, there is a way that we can harness this compulsive narcissistic approach to modern life into something that relates to their learning. Ladies and gentlemen, I give you the Wordpress blog app. A simple and easy to use app designed to be smartphone friendly as well as transferring to a tablet and desktop PC to edit or view. This app is a brilliant way of getting students to evidence reflective thoughts linking to their project work.

There are functions to use if you don't want to share the contents of the blog site with the outside world, there are also options to turn off social media sharing and comments on the sites if that would be preferred in line with your own schools ICT policies.

The main feature of this app though is the ease of documenting project work at regular stages through visual images and written text. The Wordpress dashboard can be easily accessed through a standard PC and can be edited the same as a standard IT based project in class, although there is the added benefit of being able to edit in real time online via their smartphones at home if needed to add further information and build on the content. **The other added benefit of this approach to students producing work is that you can check the progress at any point that is convenient for you without the need to take work away from them...** So, if you're the kind of person who has to juggle marking at all sorts of weird times to fit around family stuff, you can even check the reflective blogs on your phone whilst your sat at your kids Sunday football training if that's what works for you.

Try it this way...

If you are stuck in a bit of a rut in relation to exam board requirements or maybe the limitations of ICT access within the school as an assessment tool... why not try to use the blog site with older students to encourage them to create an online profile, a reflective account of their education successes with links to examples of their work, enrichment activities and work experience. This kind of approach obviously needs closely managing and rules to be set in relation to the tone and content of the information shared. However, it is a really rewarding and useful experience for the students who engage with the process.. It helps them to see the positive use of the internet aside from sharing selfies, shopping on boohoo or maybe stalking celebrities on Twitter. A really worthwhile activity to introduce at the start of KS5 in particular to encourage students to take a more active role in their future choices and consider how they sell themselves to future employers or universities.

Take a look at the exemplar 'online portfolio' used to guide my students through the process by going to:
www.mycreativeonlineportfolio.wordpress.com
or scanning the QR code

My Creative Online Portfolio

An exemplar online portfolio to support students completing UAL Art and Design qualificat

HOME   BIBLIOGRAPHY AND WEBSITES FOR REFERENCE   GALLERY VISITS AND ENRICH

INSPIRATIONAL ARTISTS   PERSONAL STATEMENT   SUPPORT FOR TUTORS   WORK

Maintaining your online portfolio

Leave a reply

The Art and Design world is an exciting and competitive place to be. The creative journey that you are on during your UAL qualification is already giving you the edge against your peers. However, it is also important that that you start to develop your own online professional presence to allow you to firmly establish yourself within the creative industry.

Use this exemplar blog site to guide and support you when developing your own online portfolio.

Top tips for blog writing..

Alternatively...

Blogs for progression and careers are something that as creatives we encourage students to engage with to build their portfolio and establish themselves as professionals in the sector... Art students are often asked now to provide a virtual portfolio of their work before being considered for interview... This is a golden opportunity to sell yourself and make a bold statement relating to what you are about. In this subject area, much the same as any other, the best way to get that much needed edge in such a competitive field (as well as gaining a credible qualification) is to build a reputation.

The use of blogging and website creation with careful guidance can give the students the ability to start to develop these skills and get ahead of the competition when applying for jobs, work experience and further education or training positions.

The ideal App for **creating your 'Brand'**

Let's just get this out there now... I do have a slight obsession with putting my face on things. Not my actual face though, it's my mini 'Bitmoji' version of my face. I know it sounds a tad vain, but there is logic behind the madness... Honest!

Bitmoji

This app allows you to create a mini digital version of yourself (an 'avatar' for those of you who are tech savvy and down with the lingo!) that you can then export and use across the full range of resources, PowerPoint presentations, posters, homework tasks sheets... The uses are endless. My particular favourite is my version of me with the wagging finger and the teacher 'death stare' - I used this one on 'see me' slips!

Whatever the use, it helps to add a little bit of 'you' into your classroom in a fun and engaging way.

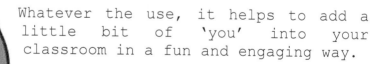

"**Why not use the app to create positive images for reward stickers? Or maybe you could add speech bubbles and use your 'mini me' to set the lesson tasks on your slideshow?"**

Keep your 'mini me' up to date by making quick edits if you get a new hair 'do', pair of glasses or suddenly decide that your outfit of choice should really be a costume from the latest film release... Personally I'm not quite sure why all schools don't encourage 'comic dress up as part of their uniform policy!

You can even edit the clothes and pop Christmas jumpers on your Bitmoji avatar... What's not to love!?

The ideal App for 'Pimping your Pictures'

If you feel a little lacking in creativity or are a little restricted with what you can present in terms of resources and materials within your subject ...that's where the subtle addition of a Polaroid edited image can add that much needed visual oomph. Edit, create and present images for use on resources. Embed things onto the power points, resources, handouts.

Use combined with other apps to create revision cards, activity cards added elements to school social media newsfeed or maybe even posters and leaflets. The choice of frames allows a range of visual effects right from modern pop colour frames with a range of corresponding fonts...

Assessment Support

Polaroid
Instant

..Through to the vintage time weathered Polaroid effect to evoke a little nostalgia.

I have to admit, this app may seem to be a bit simple and trivial in its functions... However, you must never underestimate the benefit of well-considered, well presented resource when delivering learning opportunities!
In case you haven't spotted the theme so far in this book... I'm pretty obsessed with making things look right.

Use the app to create quirky borders and frames for your images. It is so easy to use and lots of different editing options. There really is no excuse for having dull pictures on your resources ever again!

Images created can easily be saved as jpegs and into a cloud drive or directly popped into a PowerPoint slideshow/resources being created within your tablet.

Try it this way...

Why not create your own set of revision cards using images linked to the topics covered?

..Or maybe create a set of flash cards to introduce students to key topics, practitioners or theorists in your subject area?

These can be easily printed, laminated and cut into packs, popped on binding rings for ease of use as prompt cards or even use as a top trumps/matching pairs style game.

The ideal App for creating 'Exciting visual handouts'

As an art teacher one of THE most popular things that we cover, regardless of age range or artistic ability, is anything to do with the pop art movement. The bold lines, regular spot patterns, bubble writing, speech bubbles and bright primary colour combinations just seem to click with the students... I suppose that as there's a large number of products and advertisement stuff out there at the moment that embraces that retro styling of the comic book... The use of comic style resources and learning support within class is bang on trend!

You can use the app to channel your inner comic illustrator and create your own comic pop art themed resources and handouts with all of the best bits of the pop art style but without the stress of having to hand draw anything yourself... what's not to love!?

I use the app to create 'how to' guides, literacy mats as well as practical task sheets. Anything that requires a little more concentration and needs the reader to engage with the content... The comic style is brilliant for that. Even just for creating templates and page layouts for tasks, there's everything from traditional newspaper format, storyboard layouts, 'wanted' posters and the more popular marvel/DC comic layout... Complete with the ability to tweak colours, box sizes, titles, rendering etc. It's brilliant for creating simple structures to give the guidance needed for some to create a well presented piece of work... Without you having to compromise on the format that you want to use because you've downloaded it from an educational resources website as a PDF.

Try it this way…

Want to create a set of practical guides for use in class for independent working? Try creating a step by step set of instructions to guide students through a creative activity.. This allows them to problem solve and work their way through a task at their own pace.

If you are lucky enough to have class access to a set of iPads, why not ask the students to produce work on the comic life app or maybe even share the app details with your class for the next time you set a homework task... See what they create themselves using the different editing options that the app has within it. The perfect way of getting something engaging and visual produced to a high visual standard, good to give creative confidence for even the reluctant artists within your class!

Really easy editing functions within the app allow you to select your background colour, style of font and add effects to give your 'comic life' stuff that personal edge.

You can shuffle the layout around with ease to make sure that it looks exactly as you need it... Adding speech bubbles and your own images gives you so much potential for developing 'step by step' guides or maybe reference sheets for research.

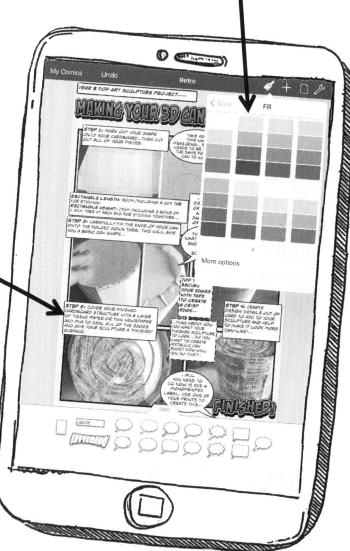

Pinterest

The ideal App for 'Visual Learning'

Pinterest is one of my favourites... Not least for the fact that it often gives some much needed respite from data and number crunching but can still be regarded as work!

As an Art teacher having the ability to collate visual images for a range of different subjects ready to tap into for new topics is invaluable. The quality of images on Pinterest is always far better than any other search engine on the interweb. It saves so much time compared with trawling through the endless tat that spews up on a regular online image search (let's face it... more time is something we often lack in this game!)

So... You may already be familiar with Pinterest as a forum for collecting recipes for making a 'cake in a mug' or maybe for finding inspiration for housewife crafting. However, it has so much more potential than that. There are 2 ways to use this app..

Try it this way ...

Create an account yourself and collect images for use on your resources, lesson planning etc. keep things nice and neat in organised boards for each topic all ready for when you need them.

Alternatively...

You could set up a Pinterest account for your subject area or department for use with students. Try creating visual inspiration for the range of projects and topics covered with each class. Use Pinterest boards as a 'go to' space for students to start research or extended learning tasks.

This approach means that you can control the images that they use for their work.

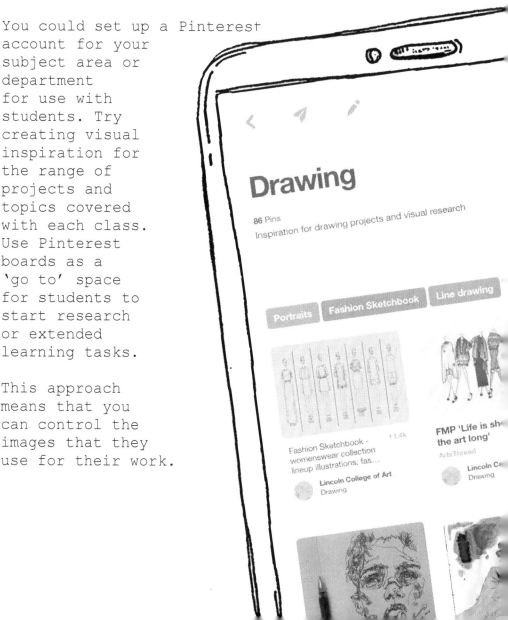

The good thing about Pinterest though is that the images the students are exposed to aren't limited to those that you select... Related images pop up underneath and allow further exploration and wider research.

Opportunities for students to create their own Pinterest account to start collecting images themselves means that they can extend their learning further and take control of their work... Perfect for open ended research tasks and coursework.

Easily accessed on a smartphone, tablet computers as well as a good old desktop PC.

Keep your images on separate boards for easy future planning.

Why not encourage students to extend their learning by creating their own Pinterest boards for research?

The ideal App for **Mixing** 'Doodles with typed text'

Noteshelf for ipad is one of those apps that does so much. Really understated but amazing. A simple app to use as an introduction to creating more quirky resources even for the creatively challenged. It can be used to simply annotate PDF files or photographs to point out the important bits... Or it can be used to create documents from scratch with a little extra creativity.

With its choice of backgrounds, fonts and ability to import images, use emoji stickers and add elements of hand drawing, this app allows you to add a little quirky edge to your written text without really even trying. The fonts are refreshingly modern and provide something that little more engaging compared to the standard text adorning education resources and text books... Just this in itself would make the worksheets, support resources and task sheets more visually appealing. You can then sprinkle a bit of colour by adding a couple of arty squiggles, diagrams, photographs (even drop a few emoji's if that's your sort of thing!)

or maybe just highlight key parts of the text to draw attention ... et voila! Instantly more engaging creative resources.

I've used this app for everything from text heavy handouts to illustration. It's simply brilliant. Noteshelf quite literally provides you with a 'shelf' on which to archive and manage your notes. A little like folders on a PC desktop. This makes the things you create far easier to manage, edit and develop.

Use the app to create a more contemporary feel to your hand outs by using different fonts... Even if you don't feel like getting particularly 'arty', use the coloured highlighters and sketching pens to emphasise particular areas of the text.

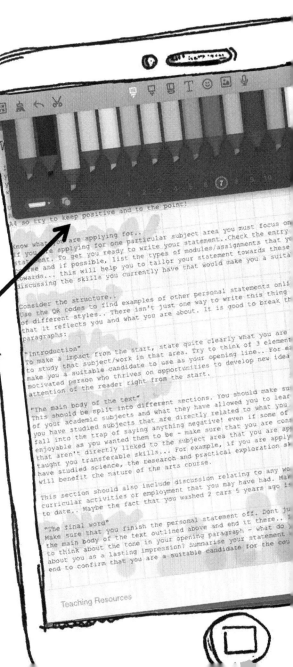

Try it this way…

Try using the app to record meeting minutes, type, highlight and doodle essential sketch notes needed to communicate the discussions and actions of the meeting. One of the best additions as a head of department is the ability to add voice recordings into the files. Create the meeting minutes and add voice recordings into the same document using the little microphone icon at the top. These can then be shared with the team for reference.

The examples of the app in use include the use of QR codes as well to add extra information into the document. The ability to save and send in a range of formats makes this app really versatile for both virtual and print format resources across your everyday planning and delivery.

Writing your personal statement

It is important that you plan well in advance of your deadline. Use your time to create draft versions of your personal statement. Ask your tutor to read through your work and provide feedback – this will allow you to get it totally right.

Use the steps below to help you to create your personal statement.. Remember, this is your opportunity to sell yourself in one side of A4 so try to keep positive and to the point!

Know what you are applying for..
If you are applying for one particular subject area you must focus on this in your statement. To get you ready to write your statement..Check the entry requirements for the course and if possible, list the types of modules/assignments that you would be working towards... this will help you to tailor your statement towards these particular courses by discussing the skills you currently have that would make you a suitable candidate.

Consider the structure..
Use the QR codes to find examples of other personal statements online. There are a range of different styles.. There isn't just one way to write this thing but you MUST make sure that it reflects you and what you are about. It is good to break the statement up into paragraphs:

"Introduction"
To make a impact from the start, state quite clearly what you are about and why you want to study that subject/work in that area. Try to think of 3 elements of your character that make you a suitable candidate to use as your opening line.. For example: "I am a creative, motivated person who thrives on opportunities to develop new ideas.." This gets the attention of the reader right from the start.

"The main body of the text"
This should be split into different sections. You should make sure that you discuss each of your academic subjects and what they have allowed you to learn/develop (particularly if you have studied subjects that are directly related to what you are applying for!) DO NOT fall into the trap of saying anything negative! even if some of your courses weren't as enjoyable as you wanted them to be – make sure that you are constructive. The subjects that aren't directly linked to the subject area that you are applying for will also have taught you transferable skills... For example, if you are applying for an arts course and have studied science, the research and practi... within science will benefit the mak...

The ideal App for 'Extended Learning Tasks'

QR code Creator

Ok... So you will have noticed already that there are lots of weird little barcode type squares within this book. Essentially that is exactly what they are.

The use of QR codes isn't a new thing, it's certainly not ground breaking in terms of technology, although it's surprising how underused they are.

It often is the case that they are pretty pointless for use in class if your school doesn't have a plethora of tablets or even a 'bring your own device' policy... This doesn't mean that they are totally pointless though. **QR codes can be used to extend learning out of class, for research or flipped learning tasks at home. Kind of like a 'Pokemon go' for the classroom if you will** (I know... I'm so down with the kids with my pop culture references!)

How it works...

There are two main parts to this: the code 'creator' app and the code 'reader' app. You can easily get both for free. The code creator allows you to create barcodes to unlock websites, images, online videos, PDF files or whatever you fancy... It's a fab way of setting homework challenges and research tasks with that extra level of intrigue. The student simply needs to use the code 'reader' app on their device to unlock the information/task/video etc.

These codes are also good used in conjunction with the other apps on this list, a way of providing further reading or background information for a topic without taking up reams and reams of paper, it makes things that little bit more interactive and hands on for the reader regardless of what age group they are.

I use them lots to provide links to the supporting Pinterest boards; YouTube clips to support the questioning task or to give links to useful websites for the subject they are studying. It allows that little extra control over where the students are accessing their research information and also gives a starting point for those who are reluctant researchers.

Try it this way...

Ways to use the QR codes in a classroom environment are endless. Some of my favourites are:

#01 In a practical workshop environment add QR codes to pieces of equipment or work stations to provide links to video demonstrations, health and safety instructions or practical tutorials.

#02 On your WAGOLL table have QR codes to unlock audio commentary to explain the visual evidence or maybe have 'how to' demonstrations to accompany the practical work.

#03 On posters around the room, add QR codes to extend the learning of a particular topic or subject. Make it a stretch and challenge task or an extension task for after they have completed the set lesson aims... Kind of like a museum with interactive activities.

Please Note: There is definitely a BIG difference between all of the QR code creators and scanners out there... You do not however need to pay money for a well behaved app. The two links below are both tried and tested apps that I use regularly:

QR Reader for iPad by TapMedia Ltdhttps://appsto.re/gb/yMTzz.i

https://play.google.com/store/apps/details?id=com.mobile.qrcodereader

The ideal App for 'Being in more than one place at a time!'

Before you get all excited, sadly I haven't discovered a cloning machine (those of you who know me will be relieved - pretty sure that one of me is enough!) neither have I got time machine/time turner or any other device to physically duplicate me.

I am talking about **using technology to start your lessons, introduce tasks and give instructions for you.** However, rather than it being in the form of a generic YouTube type clip that doesn't quite fit what you need for *your* lesson or the needs of *your* students, this is something made by you... It's easier than you might think.

Explain Everything

Using the explain-everything app you can record yourself speaking over the top of the images (photos of student work or WAGOLLS) You can even annotate and highlight areas of the slide as you are talking to draw attention whilst you are speaking.

Try it this way...

Use this method to set up self-reflection tasks, to guide students through their target setting (in a sort of meditation recording style) whilst you are able to walk around and check that students are grasping the task.

How about using it to act as a demonstration? ...Or to give basic instructions so it frees you up to distribute resources or check homework etc.

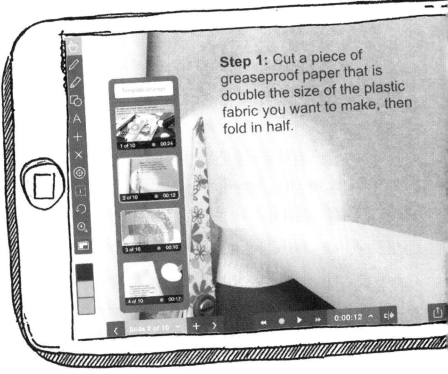

Step 1: Cut a piece of greaseproof paper that is double the size of the plastic fabric you want to make, then fold in half.

There is a big difference in engagement with the tasks set because they are being communicated via something being played in a video format... It seems to work for students

---

rather than a person standing in front of them saying the exact same thing! I guess that's a side effect of the 'YouTube generation'.

..Why not use the app for assessment feedback?

Talking through individual targets and areas for development using photographs of the students work to illustrate your comments in explain-everything will help to make the comments 'stick.' When feedback is recorded it can easily be saved as MP4 files (or even just as a visual PDF) ready to be emailed out. Students then plug headphones in to the computer/device open the email and follow the link to their own personal feedback… **It's like being in 30 places at once doing meaningful tutorials all at the same time and so much more effective than providing students with purely written feedback..** As an added bonus, they can even revisit the feedback when needed to check progress against the targets set and areas for improvement outlined in your comments.

If you're already a tablet or smartphone user... **Why not the 'virtual teacher' method to allow you to multitask to epic proportions!? Even if it's just to make you feel cool because you can control the class by just pressing play!**

The ideal App for 'Handbooks and Project Guides'

Okay... This one is a pretty self-explanatory app. The book creator app lets you create books (I know, a little obvious - but in my defense, not all apps have such an obvious title!) I've used the book creator app in a variety of ways and it's simple to use and gives maximum results.

The app has lots of different functions and is a really easy thing to use within class for students to produce evidence of their own learning... This is something that I know a lot of primary schools do fabulously to help present learning in a professional format. The same idea of professional and engaging presentation applies to resources and support materials produced by the teacher too.

Whether it be self-help revision guides, coursework survival books, subject specialist help guides for support staff and cover staff.

The possibilities are endless. I've used the book creator app to do all of these and in a variety of formats for ease of access and sharing.

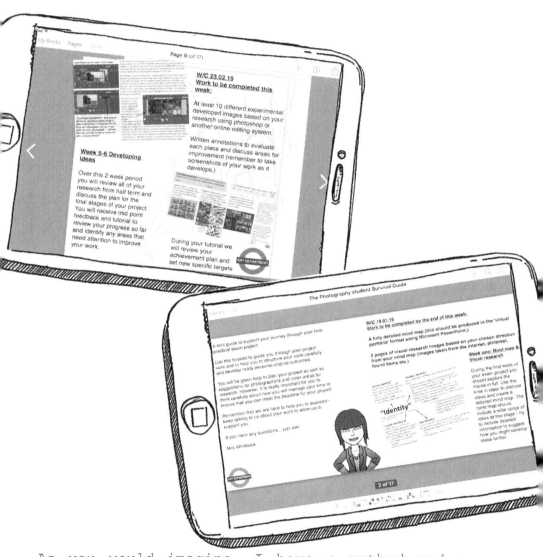

As you would imagine, I have a method and a considered way of presenting the support information within the books...

As well as the functions within the book creator editor itself, the app can easily make use of the range of other different creative apps discussed in this section to make the content of the pages work for you... Embed QR codes to link to further learning opportunities and documents or maybe pop a few Polaroid images in to create a visual focus and draw attention to key pieces of information. You can even create whole pages within your comic life app and then simply pop them into the book format... et voila! Easy engaging information book filled with whatever you want.

Try it this way...

Save the completed file as an e-book then email out to students, parents or support staff to access on their own smart phone or tablet computer. This approach is brilliant with revision guides or coursework planners in particular to help people to manage their time and workload in a way that works for them. You can include all key dates, deadlines, assessment criteria, examples of graded work, QR links to further revision and exam support etc... The list goes on. A brilliant way of keeping all stakeholders in the loop and get the results that everyone wants!

Try saving the file as a standard PDF and then producing printed booklets for use in class... A good alternative if you work in a school with limitations relating to the use of or access to smartphones and devices in class time.

The ideal App for creating 'Text over Images'

Word Swag

Unless you have managed to avoid social media you will have noticed those countless accounts on Twitter, Instagram or Facebook and the like that are dedicated to quotes pictured in stylised fonts over an arty landscape, minimalist paintbrush squiggle or maybe a stark monotone background for maximum impact.. You know the type of thing. They tend to get 'liked' lots and clutter up your newsfeed in amongst the cat pictures and the latest gossip.

These 'memes' have definitely become a go to method of communication for the youth of today (and possibly some of us older but still 'down with the kids' types too!) There is a real phenomenon and relentless thirst for communicating with images... So why not tap into the trend?

There are companies out there who have made very good money out of producing inspirational quote posters and motivational slideshows for schools. I have no doubt that there is a benefit in using such products but they do come at a cost.

WordSwag makes creating these images so simple even for the reluctant creatives out there. The bank of stock backgrounds, fonts and colours to choose from mean that you can create the correct atmosphere for your quote. **It's also really easy to create more personal branded versions by uploading jpegs with school logos on to use as your background.**

It may take a little more time than a simple cruise around YouTube or Pinterest to rehash the stuff that is out there already but making your own is well worth a try!. Give it a go, get you meme on!

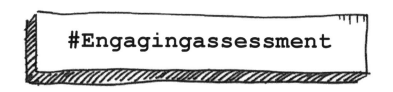

#Engagingassessment

Let's be honest, haven't we all be in this situation before, whether it be as a student or even from the other side of the fence as the teacher... Staring blankly at an overly-wordy assessment criteria grid. I'm still not sure why it is the case that exam boards and the like tend to opt for such flowery ambiguous language. **I have wondered in the past if it was a bit of a game during the specification writing process to see how many confusing words they could it into one sentence?** I imagine it to be a bit like those occasions where someone gets dared to say random words on live TV during their interview as a secret 'in' joke with fans...

Regardless of the what we are presented with to deliver, it really is important that we communicate what students are being assessed on so that they can understand how they can get there... **It's all about giving them a map to guide the way through and encourage confident exploration** (instead of them getting lost because they are trying to find their way as a result of a series of confusing riddles!)

Consider your customer...

One of the things that I uncovered whilst researching for my MA was the sheer confusion that was created by assessment criteria.. Regardless it seemed of how well the staff had tried to break things down and explain the mysteries of the grading, levels (or how they did assessment without levels!) **Crucially, the students just wanted to know how to get the marks to generally do well. Which was a relief as that's pretty much what us staff wanted too.** It all just seemed a little too much like hard work.. How on earth could the students understand how to get a good grade if they can't decipher the criteria and the tasks that are being asked of them?

This conundrum is something that many have faced in the past and I'm sure as new exam requirements and government policy changes are introduced, it will only continue. There are some cases though where we can take back control of this assessment issue... When the National Curriculum changed it gave us an opportunity to devise learning that was appropriate for *our* students. Yes, it was a slightly daunting prospect when the new subject overview for the KS3 Art curriculum was pretty much one side of A4 paper. (Especially when we compare this with the doorstop curriculum planners of the past.) How would we create 3 years of teaching and learning from that!?.. But, it was a good challenge and provided a chance for a fresh approach – To work with the students themselves to write the new plan for their learning journey...

Having developed a successful more student friendly approach to assessment in KS3 for both Design and Technology and Art with the support of student focus groups, the answer seemed clear... The best assessment systems need to make use of 'student voice' in the early stages of development to ensure they were built on solid foundations. **It's a bit like a company conducting research into their target market before creating their products.** If the customer's needs are considered in the planning stage then there is more chance of success.

Using the findings from the KS3 research and developments it was then a lot clearer to see what was needed to improve the way assessment was dealt with for the exam groups too. Even if there is quite rigid criteria set by the exam board and you don't have the luxury of being able to rewrite things... There are simple ways to help make the assessment that little bit more accessible.

This section of the book shares a few of my developed resources and methods of creating more student friendly assessment. There are also templates for you to download and edit yourself.

Student speak criteria

As an Art teacher I don't have theory exams to plan for.. That's not to say that I don't prep students for their controlled assessments and coursework with quite the same enthusiasm... Considering the confusion that often occurs when trying to explain the assessment criteria (especially when they go into 'headless chicken mode as the deadline looms!) a more considered approach is best... Thankfully, there are a few simple fixes to help regardless of your subject area.

#01 Translate

If the students look blankly at the assessment criteria offered up by the exam board..

Handy 'go to' guides with top tips for each objective

Why not translate it into words that they can relate to? You will find that there are limitations with this and the exam boards will still require you to present the 'actual' criteria to the students as well. Don't let this stop you though! By creating easy to understand versions of the assessment criteria you will find that self-assessment tasks suddenly become a lot easier as well as conversations with parents regarding progress... Even better if you can provide copies at parents evening or by email.

#02 Visualise it

Where possible include visual examples of work to help explain what the criteria is asking for. This can really help to set expectations and allow an increased level of independence. Create support sections on your resources to signpost any key tips for success.

This card supports the assessment criteria for Level 2
Unit 8: 1.1 and 1.2

PLANNING & PRODUCTION

Top Tips for doing well in this area of the criteria..

Think carefully about your technical strengths within the projects you have done throughout the year. These should form the basis of your FMP planning.
Want to know more about SWOT analysis in art and design?
Scan here or click the link below!
http://www.ualarsonportfolio.co.uk/teaching/swot-analysis-in-art-design-and-media.

Create a realistic time plan for your project. It helps if you break the time down into weeks to start with for you to then decide how you will focus your time. Think about the time that you have needed on previous projects.. Plan in enough time for research, development and making your final outcome/s.

Review your progress regularly against your time plans for the project.. if something needs to be adapted to keep you on track, speak to a tutor and agree a way forward.

UAL Level 2 FMP 'Student Speak' Assessment Support

#03 Keep them in the loop

Who do you plan for? Have you ever shared your mid- term planning in a student friendly way with your teaching groups? Why not help to keep students ready for learning by letting them in on your planning... Keep it simple though... They don't necessarily need to know how you are differentiating the tasks or embedding maths! Think about the things that they need to know to help them to be prepared for their learning. Providing the information of what is ahead helps to develop more independent and work ready learners.

#04 Make it user friendly

Okay, so it's all well and good creating endless support resources to allow students to feel 'fully prepared' for assessment.. Don't forget though that too much paper results in disengagement and 'student sleep mode.' **Us teachers might be able to sustain a lot more paperwork – but let's be honest, even we get bored by endless spreadsheets and written text.** This is how they feel when there's yet another 'important handout' to get them ready for the exam.

Try to vary the layout of your resources and consider how visually appealing they are. It may seem trivial but in a world where our youth are constantly absorbed in glossy online social media and gaming.. Sadly our resources often don't hold their attention! Try using an app to create your resource or maybe (if you're feeling a little creative) take a bit more of a brand marketing approach to create your stuff... Make things a little more visually interesting by laminating your pearls of wisdom on smaller cards and popping them on binding rings? ..A bit of effort really does go a long way when it comes to this, anything that makes the support resources 'feel' more relevant and user friendly will encourage engagement.

WAGOLL's

The thing that never seems to fail to engage the students and help them to understand how to create and improve their work every time... My WAGOLL's.

Maybe it is because I teach a practical subject, or maybe it is because students just like to be able to visualise their learning... **Kind of a Blue Peter style 'one I made earlier' approach to education?** Whatever the reason, they work.

A classroom display to enhance learning across all year groups!

When I first started using practical examples (usually a selection taken from previous students as well as my own versions of the project too) I tended to focus on the good ones - 'what a good one looks like.'

I very soon realised though that for some students, the WAGOLL made them feel that the learning was out of their grasp. On reflection, just displaying the really good examples as a positive, sort of 'ethic of excellence' or motivational learning tool within lessons made them panic. Using differentiated examples instead helped to visually explain the possible outcomes to students. In most cases, it is easy to identify the example that matches up with their own, and then look towards the next level up for inspiration. I have found that it makes no real difference what the age of the student is – using different graded sketchbooks or essays works just as well with exam groups too. Students usually feel more comfort in understanding what the next 'step up' actually looks like. Even if we do want the students to get to an 'A' grade eventually (or maybe a grade 9 depending on what exam changes have happened since publishing!), I have found that starting at a steady pace and supporting the students to improve their grade outcomes using the differentiated examples has worked better overall rather than just using 'perfect' full mark examples. I can actually genuinely say that the time spent preparing and collating examples is well worth it. The practical and visual examples drive the learning forward in my lessons; they help students to clearly understand how they can leap to the next level as well as supporting them in seeing the journey travelled by solidifying their existing knowledge through analysing the work of others.

Alternatively...

...On the flip side of this theory, I have also had lots of success using what I affectionately call a 'WACOLL' (for my own amusement of course, not necessarily shared with the kids!) ...It stands for 'what a crap one looks like.' I used this after my year 10 photographers had gone through my initial skills boot camp over the first term. To give the student's confidence in their ability I created a VERY rubbish version of their mini coursework project - I made sure that all of their little bad habits from the early stages of the course were included. Initially, they were too polite to be critical (one said she didn't want to offend me but she thought it was really rubbish!) They did soon get into the swing of it though and were able to really accurately assess the work given, before identifying the key things that they needed to avoid in their own work.

The extra bonus of using a 'WACOLL' as an alternative method of encouraging engagement with the assessment criteria is that they usually take no time at all to put together.. The idea is obviously to present an example with lots of missing bits and commonly made mistakes... Works for every subject!

Exit tickets

An oldie but still a goodie... A nice little extra to have printed out and ready to go when you have just a five minutes to consolidate the learning in your lesson.

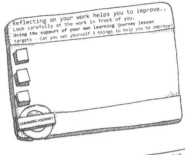

Structure the templates To make sure that you get the information that you need.

It might be a quick student voice gathering task.. Or maybe you want to know if they understood the tasks set to help you to plan for next lesson.. Use the templates to create an exit ticket that works for you.

Use their reflections to help plan next lesson...

Scan the code or click on the link below to access the 'Exit ticket templates' to edit and print yourself.

https://www.dropbox
..com/sh/6k068c9ap6p
cooy/AACU_KpeUul1KU
8TLx_TpFWUa?dl=0

Achievement Planning

I guess the easiest way to describe this is by saying it is essentially a student performance management process. It's certainly a lot more visually appealing than any performance management I've ever experienced though!

Really easy to set and review targets!

This works particularly well for groups who are working towards a long term target or final grade. It's usually easier to create a set of generic targets based on common errors or areas for improvement and then past them into the individual plan for each student. (I like to use visual prompts and WAGOLL's too to help explain the targets as well as adding links to extra places to find support.)

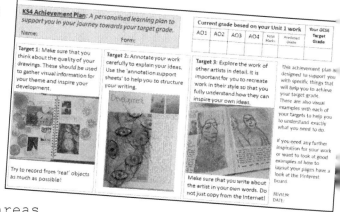

Then set the date for review – Just like a regular performance management cycle – easy!

Peer critique

Checking progress and assessing the success of a project doesn't have to just be the responsibility of the class teacher. Involving the whole group and providing structure to encourage good peer critique can give the students the feedback that they need but on their own wavelength.

I have always found that the quality of peer assessment was a little varied ...Then I realised that they didn't really appreciate why they were doing it. Peer assessment without the right ground rules and support in place can turn into a bit of a waste of time. Yes, the students will all say nice things about each other's work, which is brilliant, but doesn't push the learning forward. There is obviously a time and place for positivity but sometimes a good constructively

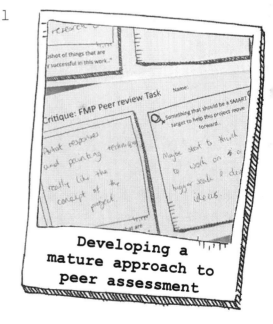

Developing a mature approach to peer assessment

critical discussion is needed. Sounds a bit much maybe? Well, this is one of those occasions where with the magic of YouTube, I let the lovely Rob Berger and 'Austin's butterfly' set the scene... Never fails me, regardless of the age group. When the scene is set, simply split the class into groups, it may be that they are naturally formed through seating plans already. Then each member of the group presents their project/ideas/theories whilst others complete the handout to provide constructive feedback for their work. This pattern then repeats until all students have presented. The golden rule is that feedback needs to be constructive and help to make improvements... like the 'Austin's butterfly' feedback. At the end of the task, each student reviews their feedback and sets SMART targets for own work based on the range of feedback they have received as well as the ideas they have seen. This task can easily be completed with post it notes (two different colours for the different types of feedback works best) but if you take the time to create your own little handout it can help give a bit more structure and guidance for the task.

Scan the code or click on the link below to access the 'peer critique templates' to edit and print yourself.
https://www.dropbox.com/sh/7bgz6au8okl1b1b/AA A8yEV_7s-Gx1cZhwxTudCBa?dl=0

Quick assessment bookmarks

Ever get the feeling that the tutorial or verbal feedback that you give goes in one ear and out of the other? ...Or maybe it gets retained but

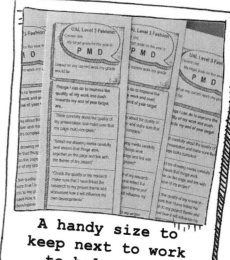

A handy size to keep next to work to help focus

not with the quite same depth and detail as is needed to inform progress. To keep my students focussed during coursework completion they were encouraged to record their feedback and check their progress towards target grades. Using a set of statements that are regularly used during summative assessments for each project (as well as the option to write other additional comments as needed) students can quickly record their area in need of development. A simple highlighting and note taking task that slots into lessons easily to support reflection and target setting... A resource to

---

Fix this into your sketchbook to help you to stay focused this week.

UAL Level 2 FMP Planning Guide
My target grade for this year is:
P M D

Think carefully about your project plan. Try to make sure that you use your time as effectively as possible.

Things I can do this week to improve the quality of my work and push towards my end of year target are...

"Present a range of recorded visual sources based on your project theme to inspire your development."

"Select my drawing media carefully and ensure that things work together on the page and link with the theme of my project."

"Check the quality of my research - make sure that I have linked the research to my project theme and discussed how it will influence my own developments."

"Add more depth into my written annotations when discussing my developing ideas – I need to be critical but constructive. Make sure that I am always looking for where I can improve."

"Check my spellings and quality of language when discussing my work. Can I use more appropriate subject vocabulary?"

Spellings that I need to correct:

Date:

Fix this into your sketchbook to help you stay focused this week.

UAL Level 2 FMP Weekly Target
My target grade for this year is:
P M D

Think carefully about your project. Try to make sure that you use you as effectively as possible.

Use the space below to yourself targets for t When setting your targ consider how well you a the assessment criteri project.

Peer/tutor feedback on my work:

Date:

adapt to suit the needs of your group or project structure. These are a good way to bookend a period of independent project work within a lesson too; targets set can be reviewed at the end to check progress. The feedback sheets are in the form of bookmarks and easily slot into workbooks rather than an A4 sheet that often gets folded, filed and not referred to again. The more hand held student friendly bookmark format has proved to be more accessible for those who have used them.

Try it this way...

#01 Create 'success criteria' bookmarks based on the homework that you set for your group... Then use them for peer assessment at the start of the next lesson. A quick way to allow students to understand if they have met the criteria before they leave the lesson.

#02 Differentiate your bookmarks, try to think about how *your* groups will engage with them... if you want to use them for peer or self-assessment.. Try using a little more structure. More able groups may prefer a bit more empty space to write their feedback.

Scan the code or click on the link below to access the 'Quick feedback templates' to edit and print yourself.
https://www.dropbox.com/sh/eb5kkn9vuxwc1iw/AACyD0webvXMEFEP-C87JJ0ca?dl=0

#Celebrateandshare

Ok... so, as you may have gathered by now, there's often lots of exciting things to celebrate and share when you think a little differently and teach the #Quirkyclassroom way. As you would imagine, there's also a 'quirky' way to do this bit too ...This section of the book shares the little tricks I have found successful to get the students on board and start to think in a positive way about their work. They are nothing earth shatteringly hard or too time consuming... Just little tweaks and templates will help to get that 'buy in' needed to keep the good stuff going.

Note: Positivity is contagious and often develops into a whole school pandemic infecting staff and students. You have been warned.

Making it relevant...

One of the golden rules of creating any kind of reward system within a school environment is making is relevant to the people receiving the rewards. **Just because I like sticky notes doesn't mean that my students are going to like them as rewards**... although I have to say, in my experience most of my students have surprised me in the past by getting as excited as me about the bright blue speech bubble shaped sticky notes magpied from the supermarket! .. Bless them. I trained them well.

In the current days of ever decreasing education budgets and limited resources for buying physical objects or vouchers for use as school rewards – **We need to think a little more creatively** about how we do the little things to boost self-esteem, celebrate the successes and generally create that 'feel good' factor around your subject area.

I'm sure I am not the only one who has seen enthusiastic well-meaning (often costly) attempts by staff to celebrate the success of students resulting in a 'cringe thing' that no student would want to receive EVER... Just for the simple fact that no one stopped to think whether the process was pitched right for the people on the receiving end of the process, the 'customers.'

All of the ideas on the following pages work across all age groups and are easy enough to tweak according to your needs.

#Sketchbookselfie

How to get them to..
'Take pride in their work'

There are so many occasions where such good work is produced in school and it never leaves the safe protection of the exercise book it was created in.. Well, at least not until the end of the year when everything gets brought home and then piled into a big box under a bed/on top of the wardrobe etc.

There have often been times when my classes would beg to take their precious case bound sketchbook home to 'show and tell' what they had done in class that day... This often made me VERY nervous (and sometimes, depending on the individual, I agreed.) As with other subjects, we had special books for assessment evidence that followed them through the whole of KS3 that were meant to stay at school. The thought of them leaving the classroom caused the panic to set it... "What if they lost the book?" Or "What if their blackcurrant juice bottle leaked all over a whole academic years' worth of work when they were transporting it home!! Aarrgh!!... Nightmare!"

Now, even though my slight control freak nature was evidently an issue with this scenario, it was a genuine problem that students weren't easily able to take pieces of work home to share and allow parents to see what they had been doing. **This spawned an idea... and so the #sketchbookselfie was born.**

Simply popping one of the 'selfie' stickers on the front of their books gave them the opportunity to request for work to be captured and shared via email with parents.

Labels are available as both a PDF and an editable publisher file by scanning the QR code here or following the link below:
https://www.dropbox.com/sh/ytxmap9b8wafgqr/AAA35Oh MYZVcMHGyLUhqQhLRa?dl=0

All the student has to do at the end of the lesson is doodle a little camera in the corner of their work. This then tells you to photograph and email home to parents.
It was often surprising to see who and what the students would request to share.. It's easy to forget that each individual finds different things challenging and exciting throughout the different subjects.
The #sketchbookselfie provides a good opportunity to open a positive dialogue with home and allow you to share the good stuff.

Try it this way...

#01 In addition to sharing the image of the work with parents via email, why not take the opportunity to share upcoming events, homework tasks and set the context of the project? Just type out a generic paragraph and copy/paste into each email. A really simple way of passing useful information on at the same time.

#02 Why not share the images in an online forum? Use the schools own website or VLE to showcase the work produced. If your school is a bit more into the social media stuff.. Ask if the images can be shared online to a wider audience too.

#03 Take ownership and make the sharing selfie yours.. Make the little tweaks needed for your groups or your subject.. Why not change the name and edit the labels to fit your department? How about a #Scienceselfie or maybe a #Schoolworkselfie

How to get them to...
'Be bothered about homework'

Now... There's lots of genius ideas and creative ways to make homework that little bit more interesting. I fully endorse anything that makes your groups get enthusiastic and generally 'see the point' in doing it... Whether you go for a 'take away' menu style of delivery, prefer the flipped learning approach or maybe opt for a longer more in depth full half term project to extend the learning at home.. As long as it works for you and your school and ultimately helps to push their learning.

I don't know about you, but the one thing that I have always had issues with has been getting the homework in on time. Yes, if your school has the policy to issue detentions etc. for non-submission then this has to be part of your plan of attack..

Let's be honest, sometimes there are just more positive ways to deal with persistent 'non-homeworkers' though that have more of an impact. In my experience detentions and sanctions alone won't change the culture.

Homework Loyalty Card

Try to put yourself in their shoes to help fix the culture... Adopt a positive approach to reinforce the importance of homework within your classroom. Simply using a stamp card (like those issued by coffee chains) each time homework is submitted on time to allow rewards to be given out to 'loyal learners.'

Try setting the challenge over the course of a half term with little prizes for the first students to complete 2 rows, a full card etc. All it needs to work is for you to promote it and spark all of those competitive feelings that kids get when they know they are collecting stuff... Whether its football stickers, Pokemon cards, POGs (oh my.. remember those!?) this system works just the same.

Download your editable template for the loyalty cards by scanning this QR code or by following the link below:

https://www.dropbox.com/sh/h1og6yfrygeh6c7/AAD jusJ6VCaCZigi4icVMga7a?dl=0

Try it this way...

Why not adapt the cards to reward helpfulness in class? I had my own 'Whitelock points' cards complete with my Bitmoji character on... Points rewarded for students who washed up and kept the classroom tidy.

How to get them to...
'Want to be on the wall'

Ben Whitelock Year 4

Celebration Selfie

Trying to think of different ways to create 'celebration walls' around school can be a challenge and often a costly venture...

I have seen some flipping AWESOME gallery style spaces with all manner of gold sprayed frames and huge digitally printed banners... All very fabulous and totally brilliant. However, if costs are in need of being as low as possible but you still want to celebrate and share the individuals who have been generally AMAZING it can feel a little bit of an impossible challenge. **Try to think back to basics, think about what they actually want... This is where the humble selfie comes in.**

Never ceases to amaze me how the youth of today are generally quite obsessed with daft poses, snapchat filters and anything to do with a 'selfie.' Why not embrace this and create your next 'student of the term' notice board with selfie style images? Allow them to pull the daft faces, add props and signs to help them to feel some ownership for the images going up on the wall. You'd be surprised how keen they are to pose... The #bluesteel (pictured above) is optional.

Try adding quirky frames using your Polaroid app as well as accessorising the display with speech bubble cut outs to explain why the 'selfie' got onto the wall.

If you have a digital screen why not create a slideshow of images and have it rotating around. This option is particularly good if you want to issue rewards regularly without having to overhaul the displays on your noticeboards every time. This option also gives the added chuckle value of it looking a lot like that moment in Ant and Dec's Saturday Night Takeaway when they scroll through the photos of the audience members to select a contestant to 'play the ads' ...Another simple way to make the celebration stuff relevant to the students at no extra effort.

..Try it this way

Want to get a little bit more creative with your celebration display? Why not use the 'speech bubble template' to create your own photo booth props? Lots of possibilities to personalise the text and make it truly relevant to you and your students.

How to make your 'photo booth selfie prop'...

Step 1...Get ready to make

You will need...
BBQ kebab sticks
Scissors
Laminator & pouches
(Yay... laminating!)
Sticky tape
Cheap white labels
Printed templates
click on the link below or scan the QR code to get the speech bubble template for your selfie stick.

https://www.dropbox.com/sh/v0jn5wgw2mui214/AACuB-ZCXcJR79G23Rf4QMtYa?dl=0

Step 2: Once edited and printed, laminate all of your speech bubbles.

I recommend that you do this with the aid of a glass of something and take advantage of the calm process of the laminator doing its thing... and relax!

Step 2... laminating

Step 3... Cut your bubbles out

Step 3: Equally as relaxing... Now you will need to cut around the laminated bubbles. Personally I like to spread them all out when done and admire the neatness... this part is optional though.

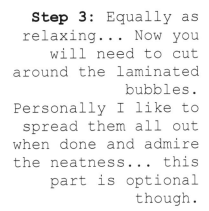

Step 4... Fix the stick with tape

Step 4: Attach your skewers to the reverse of your bubbles using a piece of tape... pointy end at the top.

Step 5... Secure with a label

Step 5: place a large label over the end of the stick. This secures everything in place and also helps to hide the sharp bits!

"et Voila!"

..And then you're ready to go! #selfie

How to get them to...
'Feel appreciated'

You don't need me to tell you that a little positivity goes a long way. One tried and tested method of sharing positive messages with home is by using praise postcards. Not a particularly revolutionary method of celebrating success, but a solid 'go to' for lots of teachers across the country each term. Postcards are sent, and proudly stuck on the fridge by parents ready to provide a point of conversation to anyone that pops around for a brew. Now, I wonder how many of those postcards promptly get photographed and shared on the various social media sites by the proud parents?.. too many to count I'm sure. In a world where everything is virtual and people share so much of their 'good news' stuff on social media, why don't we take advantage and do more virtual sharing at school?

 **The resources and templates available by scanning the QR code or by clicking on the link below will allow easy editing for the range of applications in this section:**

https://www.dropbox.com/sh/3k2si8nub1t97qt/AAAXId-KQl_pKVXQBZiISEyFa?dl=0

Benefits of going virtual...

By creating an 'e-card' style message and emailing parents the image can be instantly shared as they please, extra promotion for the

school as well as an obvious cost saving for the school as well with there being no need for stamps!

The templates on the link give you everything you need to create your own e-cards. Simply pop a school logo in the corner and add a 'well done' message of your choice in the centre... save the file as a JPEG and then attach to your email.

If you don't fancy going virtual just yet... why not edit the template and create your own postcards for printing and posting instead? Use thin white card to print your very own double sided postcard design.

Try it this way...

Praise Postcards

Everyone likes to be appreciated... Why not use the 'thank you teacher' templates or create your own for use at the end of the academic year to help students show their appreciation?

Alternatively, these also make nice 'well done' messages from SLT after special events or after observing some particularly awesome stuff on a learning walk.

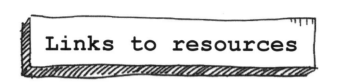

Awesome app examples:
https://www.dropbox.com/sh/s11xmq8oe0khhzi/AAC
_-1HT20L2IrhITF3g9a_ra?dl=0

Engaging assessment:
https://www.dropbox.com/sh/ymexbmh6nfllnk6/AAB
TXTaczah2WhS3tiC-TFbda?dl=0

Literacy Games:
https://www.dropbox.com/sh/esk0b846zgrt8au/AAC
nen7vix2FpTT7ZjoRX7w5a?dl=0

Literacy Mat Examples:
https://www.dropbox.com/sh/a2imellaz0c7bv3/AAC
S0hL5Nbmw_UboBhWReMmva?dl=0

Celebrate and Share:
https://www.dropbox.com/sh/9e7d22t0lr5w1ac/AAB
qCODePWtnWoYC0y-TnhNUa?dl=0

Contact

I would love to know how you have used the ideas and resources in this book.. and to see the range of uses for the templates and ideas. Sharing ideas helps to create that inspiration spark for others. Let's keep the #Quirkyclassroom conversation going and help to promote more of the positive chat in relation to teaching and learning!

If you are happy for me to share and re-tweet your ideas on Twitter please pop me a little message through on @mrsartytextiles with photographs if possible to help others to see how you have done the #Quirkyclassroom thing!

A few 'thank you' messages

Firstly, for you reader.. Thank you to you for purchasing this book – If you have managed to get to the end then **in my opinion you deserve a laminated certificate for enduring my ramblings.. Well done!**

Thank you for the patience and enthusiasm of **all of my students past and present** who have allowed me to test out my slightly bonkers approach to teaching.

Thank you also to **my supportive colleagues both in my day job as well as the virtual staff room on Twitter.** Thank you for tolerating my silly ideas, the constant (seemingly never ending) discussion of 'when the book will be finished' as well as my over excitement when the laminator gets switched on! There are too many people to mention individually, but you know who you are x